SWEET AROMA OF SUCCESS

7 Motivational Guidelines to Success

DR. ORAL HAZELL

Contents

1. Dedication
2. Acknowledgements
3. About the Author
4. Chapter One
5. STIR UP YOUR DREAMS AND YOUR DESIRES TO SU
6. CHAPTER TWO
7. Destined For Greatness
8. CHAPTER THREE
9. SMELL THE AROMA OF SWEET SUCCESS
10. CHAPTER FOUR
11. TIME IS MONEY
12. CHAPTER FIVE
13. SUCCESS SPEAKS TO ME
14. CHAPTER SIX
15. MOVE TO REALIZE YOUR DREAM
16. CHAPTER SEVEN
17. BE LIKE THE CACTUS
18. MY CLOSING THOUGHTS

SWEET AROMA OF SUCCESS

7 Motivational Guidelines to Success

BY

Dr. ORAL HAZELL

All scripture quotations are from the King James Version of the Bible unless otherwise indicated.

Copyright © 2009 by Oral Hazell

Contact information:

If you would like to have Rev. Dr. Oral Hazell as a guest speaker in your church or conference. Please contact our office at 340-774-5400 Monday-Friday between the hours of 9-5 or e-mail us at oralhazellgloballife@gmail.com

All rights reserved. Written permission must be secured from the publisher to use, quote, or reproduce any part of this book, except for brief quotations in critical review or articles.

First printing, July 2009

Second printing, June 2010

Printed in the United States of America

Published By

Brentwood Christian Press

www.BrentwoodBooks.com

1-800-334-8861

Dedication

This book is dedicated to my beloved and indefatigable mother, Norma Hazell.

Acknowledgements

My thanks to all those who assisted me in the development of this book. Thank you for your editorial work in the preparation of the manuscript: Ramona Whitehurst, Kimberly Ritter, Diane George, Charmaine Pratt, Maxine Anderson, Simonia Athanase-Dagou and Evelyn Turnbull.

My special thanks to my dear wife, Everine Turnbull Hazell, for her constant love and support.

About the Author

Pastor Oral F. Hazell, the son of a preacher, lives in St. Thomas, United States Virgin Islands. Pastor Hazell is the senior pastor and founder of Global Life Church, a spirit-filled, charismatic church that focuses on evangelism and prayer.

Pastor Hazell is a graduate of Victory Bible Institute in Tulsa, Oklahoma. He studied business at the United Business College in Miami, Florida. He also studied journalism, writing and business communications at Trans World College in the United Kingdom. In 2003, Pastor Hazell received an honorary Doctor of Divinity degree from Canon College and Seminary and Bible College. Pastor Oral Hazell was awarded a Masters of Arts in Christian Ministries, and a Bachelor of Arts Degree in Biblical Studies.

A visionary with an apostolic and prophetic anointing, Pastor Hazell has often declared that his dream is "to be a spiritual catalyst who births revival in the Caribbean!" His vision is to birth one million prayer intercessors worldwide.

As a pastor, teacher, evangelist, powerful intercessor, motivational speaker, poet and writer, Pastor Hazell is a multi-gifted man of God who addresses critical issues affecting every aspect of human, social and spiritual development. The man of God often addresses significant current issues on the radio and via electronic media.

He ministers the word and teaches at conferences in the Virgin Islands, and throughout the Caribbean Islands such as: Trinidad, Tortola, St. Kitts, Grenada, Anguilla, St. Martin, and St. Lucia. He also has ministered in the United States and Africa.

Pastor Hazell is married to Everine Turnbull Hazell, and they are the blessed parents of a beautiful daughter, Nia.

Chapter One

STIR UP YOUR DREAMS AND YOUR

DESIRES TO SUCCEED

YES, YOU CAN KICK CANNOT OUT OF YOUR LIFE! Today!

PICTURES PEOPLE PAINT OF YOU

AFFIRMATION: I determine today that I will wash my mind of negativism. I will think positive thoughts. Today, I will surprise those who thought or said negative thoughts towards me. I will arise from the doldrums and walk in my destiny. Today, I will release positive charges, which will get me into my destiny.

Now, you are a dreamer and you happened to share your dream with someone. They responded with something negative. During the writing of this book I told a good friend of mine that I was writing a book. He laughed hysterically in a negative way. Maybe someone told you or made you feel as if you will never be a success. That something may be transfixed in your mind. You may be meditating on it. If you begin to meditate on it, not only are you repeating the negative concept of the words that person spoke to you, but you are acting it out.

The stages of Negative Words

1. Negative words are vocalized by someone.

2. It is heard by an individual.

3. The words enter the individual's subconscious mind.

4. The words are then repeated in the mind.

5. The words are then acted out.

6. The words paint a picture or create **a positive** or **negative inner image** of you.

Now let us look into each listing. First, negative words are vocalized by someone. The person may be someone who has had negative experiences or influences in their life. These people are called pessimists. Their job on earth is to propagate negativism. Every idea you can conjure up, they respond to it negatively, "It cannot be done or it will never be done." These types of people try to belittle you by saying things that will immediately affect your mindset. They will tell you that the idea you have cannot work as long as the world is in existence.

Secondly, the words are heard by you. The words travel into the air, then into your ear. Then they travel down into the inner ear, which leads into your mind. This area controls your emotions. The words spoken can often traumatize you immediately depending on how the words were spoken. I remembered very vividly while I was attending school that an enemy of mine told me that I had big thick lips. I was immediately dehumanized and felt that I was an ugly fellow. I was now made aware of my thick lips. I would look into the mirror and strum them with my fingers like someone playing a bass guitar. My self esteem fell to about 40 on a scale of 100. I had very little self esteem left.

Thirdly, the negative words enter your subconscious mind. It is in the subconscious mind where constant repetition occurs. There, you rehearse the words that were spoken by the negative person, creating a pygmy image, a loser image, a lazy image, a no purpose image and a do nothing image. It is in your subconscious mind that images of yourself are created. Your ideas and your dreams are created and stored in your subconscious mind. They also are developed and arranged in sequence. For example, if you hear the infamous phrase, "You will never amount to anything," and you allow that to stay in your subconscious mind and mediate on it, you will eventually reproduce what you are meditating on.

Four, the negative words are repeated or mused upon. Negative words that are mused upon stop you from fulfilling your destiny or your purpose on earth. Words spoken to you by your mother or father, such as "You will never amount to anything," "You are lazy," "You are a bum," can be stagnating because your mind is like the cow's stomach. The food travels through the omasum, then to the abomasum. It is then regurgitated by the cattle, by chewing its cud. The food travels from these chambers back into the mouth where all the juices are extracted by the cow's chewing, bringing health and nourishment to the cow. This also happens when we receive negative words. They eat at you and give you a putrid feeling. You tend to see failure before you have failed. You see death or taste death before you die. Repetition on the negative gives you the feeling that all is lost. Then you do the proverbial; throw up your hands and quit. Negative words that are allowed to take root in your subconscious mind lead to lost potential and an early grave.

Fifth, negative words are acted out. Words are carriers of negative or positive stimuli of success or failure. They can carry fresh water or putrid water. Words spoken bring success or encourage failure. You act out the words that are heard and the words that are seated in the subconscious. Have you ever had someone call you stupid? Then when you were in the presence of that individual you acted stupid. You were acting out that person's thought pattern of you. Your reaction was a negative catalyst. So if someone were to call you a thief [big negative] chances are they will catch you stealing, or on the positive if they called you trustworthy, chances are that your character will be developed to that of a person of integrity.

Sixth, the negative words spoken paint an inner image inside you. The image you see in your inner self determines what you portray to other people. This is a very critical point. You teach people to treat you in a certain manner, because the image you portray will reflect and accentuate a response from the people around you. If you release negative vibrations you will receive a negative response from people. So today, determine to look positive and walk with your head up and your shoulders squared. It is your day to exude the positive.

POWER POINT

"I determine today that I will wash my mind of negativism. I will think positive thoughts. Today I will surprise those who thought or said anything negative towards me. I will arise from the doldrums and walk in my destiny. Today, I will release positive charges."

MEDITATION SCRIPTURES

"I know the thoughts that I think toward you, saith the Lord, thoughts of peace, and not evil, to give you an expected end."

Jeremiah 29:11

POINTS TO REMEMBER

1. It is in the subconscious mind that constant regurgitation occurs.

2. Negative words that are mused upon shrink you up, belittle you. They stop you from fulfilling your destiny and your purpose.

3. Words are carriers; words are like a bucket. They carry fresh water or words that will dehumanize you. Words spoken encourage success or encourage failure.

CHAPTER TWO

Destined For Greatness

Affirmation: Everyone is destined for greatness. I was created to accomplish a task. I will not die before that task is accomplished. Today, I will leave this world better than I met it.

Like a seed you are filled with potential. You might be at a dormant stage in your life, obscured from everyone. You may be depressed and even thinking about giving up; thinking about quitting-breathing your last breath.

Your life, like a seed has stages. The seed, when placed in the right environment, starts releasing its potential. A seed has the potential to become a 300 foot pine tree but if it is not in the correct environment it will not soar high to greet the sunlight and bathe it's leaves in the first rain. The pine tree will not be able to release its potential in providing mankind with its timber. The seed, like your life, when it is released into the correct environment takes on a different image. Growth begins to take place. The plant begins to change its environment. If there was a rock placed on it, it would move the rock or the tree system will meander. The plant will bear leaves, flowers and fruit, and will give shade to its surroundings.

Like the plant, you can change your environment. Decide not to stay dormant any longer, but to move into that environment that will foster change, today, not tomorrow. Remove any stone or stubble that is in your path. Begin your growth process, now by forgetting the past. Do not let your past dictate your future nor rule your present. Forget the blame-game trips that you take everyday. Forgive and forget and move on with your life. Most successful people become successful because one day they decided, without any resolve, to be focused with determination, that there will be no looking back or going back. They will accomplish their heart's desire and realize success.

You must become fed up of living the mediocre life and get into the lane of productivity and purpose. Decide today that you are destined for greatness; no matter what the obstacles may be. Resolve that you will remove obstacles. You will sink your roots down deep and live a fruitful and productive life in order to bring about change in your life, your family, your community, your church and your world.

If you are going to grow, you must become secure. This is when you need faith that you can bring about change in your life. Faith, not in yourself, but in the Creator. The Creator, who has placed faith in you, can make anything happen in your life. There are times when you will do the impossible. You may be afraid, but you will do it anyhow. You must cross your Red Sea of fear and uncertainty to get to your promised land.

Many people do not want to grow. They act like a parasite, living off of every one around them, parents, friends and bosses.

You must decide that you will grow, and your life, like the seed, will start giving out what is inside. You will start giving out that fragrance filled with the flower of success that others, like bees, will come and drink of your nectar. You will give shade, (protection) and inspiration to others, that they too can grow tall and reproduce after their kind. Like the plant, when you have expired, you would have completed your life's goal. You would have left a legacy and an inheritance behind.

Resolve today with that focused determination that you will leave this world in better shape than you found it. Yes you can do it. Today, leave your mind printed on the minds of men and women. Yes, you can!

POWER POINT

I am destined for greatness. Today, I will wholeheartedly resolve to make a difference in my world to better mankind.

MEDITATION SCRIPUTRE

"Whatsoever thy hand findeth to do, do it with thy might; for there is no work, nor device, nor knowledge, nor wisdom, in the grave, wither thou goest."

Ecclesiastes 9:10

POINTS TO REMEMBER

1. Like a seed you are filled with potential.

2. Like a plant you can change your environment and your destiny.

3. Do not let your past dictate your future success.

4. You need faith in yourself and faith in the Creator to bring forth change.

5. Resolve today to leave the world in a much better shape than you met it.

6. Do not let your past dictate your future nor rule your present.

7. You must become fed up of living the mediocre life and get into the lane of productivity and purpose.

CHAPTER THREE

SMELL THE AROMA OF SWEET SUCCESS

Affirmation: You cannot look at putrefying garbage and see the rose-filled garden of success. I decide today to look into the right places to see the right things.

So many people are looking in the wrong places to find peace of mind and inspiration. If you want to change the state you are in, you will have to do something that you have never done before to bring forth change in your life and then change in your surroundings. You must experience change, and then others around you can change. You then become the liberator of others.

Change can come about in your life today. You have control of your destiny, only you. Say, "I have control over my destiny today." Say it out loud or you can screech it out loud in your spirit. Now and only now can you take charge of your life. You may have been missing a few mundane things in your life. You may be thinking that you have been born into the wrong family (remember we cannot choose our parents). You may have lived your life dependent on someone else. You may have even been adopted into the wrong family. Now is the time to change. Answer this question: Do you want to see change in your life now?

Circle yes or no.

If yes, read on. The mere fact that you are reading this book shows that you thirst for change in your life, in your family's life, in your community, village and country. Do you know that within you lies all the abilities to forge change in your life? Change begins with a start. Make that first step towards change in your life. Literally surprise yourself into change. Do not spend your life resisting change. Many people spend all their life resisting change. You are changing everyday. Therefore, since you are changing every day encourage change mentally, educationally and spiritually. When the men landed on the moon on July 20, 1969, many people resisted it even though it was a fact and they saw it happening on the television screen.

Now you have to look in the right places. How about that dream you had since you were a youth? What has happened to that dream? Did that dream die? Why do you think it has died? It has died for lack of perseverance or maybe you have tried working towards your dream, then it became thwarted because of some miscalculation. Further on in the book, I will show you how to persevere until you have attained your goal. Then you will be able to live the fruitful life, fulfilling your purpose in this journey of life here on the earth.

Look in the right places. You may have to start looking at the successful people in the community. I remember working for Mr. Finch, who was a very successful man in our neighborhood. I worked with him for six months in his department store and he changed my life. He suggested to me that I should read Napoleon Hill's success books. Then I got hooked. I am now an avaricious reader of success oriented books and autobiographies. Mr. Finch was my motivator.

Find out where successful people frequent and work at being in their company. Find out how they think. I can assure you that this breed thinks differently than the average person. Find out what they are doing and what you are not doing. Yes, this strategy can cause you to rise from the grimy pile of failure and catapult you into success, by knowing the right people who have good, sound ideas and a plan to make their ideas work. You might have to do some homework, but you must work to achieve your goals. So now, decide to take an about face and look into the direction of success. How much do you want it? Are you hungry for success? Go for it. Stop looking where you are looking. Obviously, you have not found it in the direction that you are presently looking.

You may have to start reading motivational books and listening to motivational tapes. Just shut out all the negative people. Decide today that you will experience the successful life. You were wired by the Creator to be successful. So, within you is that seed that wants to germinate and blossom to its full potential of success.

Decide today to stop looking on the garbage heap of failure, procrastination, negativism, rejection, and self-pity. Rather, choose to look on the rose garden of life, blooming with multicolor roses of success – smell the aroma of success.

POWER POINT

I refuse to look on the putrefying garbage of life. I choose to turn my gaze and look on the blooming roses of success. I smell and see success. It is tangible and I can feel it.

MEDITATION SCRIPTURE

"This book of the law shall not depart out of thy mouth; but thou shalt meditate therein day and night, that thou mayest observe to do according to all that is written therein: for then thou shalt make thy way prosperous, and then thou shall have good success."

Josh.1:8

POINTS TO REMEMBER

1. Do something you have never done before to change the state that you are now in.

2. Today, become the liberator of others as you experience change in your life.

3. You have control of your destiny.

4. Change begins with a start.

5. Surprise yourself into change today.

6. Know the right successful person, who can turn you on to do the right things.

7. Decide today that you will experience the successful life.

CHAPTER FOUR

TIME IS MONEY

Affirmation: Today, I determine to use my time wisely. I will do only things that will reproduce success in my life – things that will produce happiness, health and wealth. Today, I seize the moment. I seize the time. I plan to succeed and work my plan.

Until you get angry, sick and tired of what you are, you will not change. Until you get sick, frustrated and disgusted with how you are living your life in the daily, mundane activities, you will just trudge along and live your life like the other people around you. However, if you really want to see change, irreversible change in your life, you must become dissatisfied with living to the everyday drum beat of this life.

If you want to see change, you and only you can orchestrate change in your life. It is only you who can get up tomorrow, get a piece of paper and start setting goals and objectives for your life. Are you angry? Yes, you ought to be angry with yourself for being a 33 year old couch potato (you can substitute your age) just looking at your television set night and day. Have you ever wondered how much money the people you are watching in a movie make? Now, do not get me wrong. I am speaking to those who have no self control. It is good to have a few hours of television a day, but when you spend your entire evenings during the week just looking at the television set you are in need of self control.

After you have done your regular job, what do you do with your spare time? How you use your spare time determines if you are pursuing the successful life. Nothing motivates us more than constant exposure to success. Therefore expose yourself to life's success. One avenue is to read information on what you want to pursue now in your life. The more informed you are the more proficient you will be in your pursuits.

Today, you can earn a fortune if you will take advantage of time and are willing to pay the price of hard work. Time is your most valuable asset. Time coupled with a plan and a strategy to fulfill your plan equals success. Time lost can never be regained. However, time lost can be redeemed by using the time that you have now to your advantage. Remember that tomorrow's time is not wasted.

Tomorrow is fresh, ready to work for you! You can turn over a new leaf, tomorrow. One thing you must remember is that you are getting older and time is passing you by. Do not allow yourself to say, "I could have owned that business or that mansion." You are preoccupied with the little things, while the big things are passing you by. Take action now and seize your moment and pursue your dream.

The proper use of time in your life now will guarantee you freedom, happiness and success in your lifetime. Therefore, start now to use your time wisely. It is said that we have been created equal; we have been given the same beautiful 24-hour day, the same night; the same day. However, it is those that seize the moment in time that will benefit in the future. Spend the necessary time developing yourself and spend time at the business of your dream and choice. Work until the job is done correctly or you are pleased, and the person you are serving is pleased.

Yes, you can earn a fortune. Today, or in the future, if you just take control of your twenty-four hour day. Great achievers and successful people all have one thing in common: They have learned to take control of their time. Remember that time is translated into money. Therefore, any time you waste doing nothing to cultivate your mind or to pursue your goal, just add the time wasted multiplied by the money you made on your daily job. You will be surprised that the time wasted can be calculated into millions.

To succeed in life, you must have a plan. If you do not have a plan, you are planning to fail. Set a time to start working on your plan – to make a plan. No plan is a failed plan. However, if you have a plan on how you are going to use your time, you will be gaining momentum toward achieving success in your pursuit. People who are out of control, I encourage you to set up a time table showing every hour of your day. Completely follow it for the first six months of the year. Then, for the last six months give yourself a little more leisure time. Then watch the remarkable change that will come over your life. With this plan I believe you can pursue your life's purpose.

POWER POINT

Today I determine to use my time wisely. I do only the things that will reproduce success in my life; things that produce Happiness, Health and Wealth. Today, I seize the moment and seize the time. I plan to succeed and work my plan.

MEDITATION SCRIPTURE

"I can do all things through Christ who strengthens me."

Philippians 4:13

POINTS TO REMEMBER

1. Nothing motivates us more than constant exposure to success.

2. The more informed you are, the more you will be proficient in your pursuits.

3. Time is your most valuable asset.

4. Remember that tomorrow's time is not wasted.

5. Do not be preoccupied with the little things while the big things are passing you by.

6. The proper use of time in your life now will guarantee you freedom, happiness and success in your lifetime.

7. Work until the job is done correctly.

8. To succeed in life, you must have a plan and work the plan.

CHAPTER FIVE

SUCCESS SPEAKS TO ME

(This chapter came to me in a dream. It is in proper poetry form)

Affirmation: I will listen to the sweet sound of success. I will let it guide me. I will forget past mistakes and past failures. Success is my guide today.

I would like to tell you this story of a land you can reach. A place where there are only a few. A land that is perfect and sublime. Few people get there because they are not disciplined and they are afraid (they are afraid to come on this journey with me). As I take them to this land; that oh only a few strugglers get to. The land that mushrooms with health, wealth, peace of mind and contentment. Yes, you too, can get there in that perfect place of rest.

The perfect place of rest is not far away. It walks with you and communes with you. But oh, will you take the time to listen? It is that place you always wanted to attain – a place of wealth, status, success and the happy life. Yes, it is not far away. Listen, it is so close to you. It screams every day but are you listening? Are you listening? It touches you everyday and you take it off like a piece of rag, but it touches you everyday.

Success is around you but you do not want to see it. You are so comfortable in the rut you are in. It is time for a change. It is time to do the unthinkable, the unimaginable for your life TODAY, not tomorrow. You can if you stretch beyond the limitations of your mind. Work! Let work become play and your exercise each day. Then you will find comfort and success in the things that you do each day to bring gain to yourself and satisfaction and pride to others. I, Success, speak to you. I, Success, say to you that you can achieve through day and night, through the wind, the heat and the cold, and through life's stormy seas. I, Success, say to you that you can touch me, you can sleep with me, you can live every day with me, and you can reach my land, IF YOU ONLY PERSEVERE. I, Success, await your arrival.

POWER POINT

I will listen to the sweet sound of success. I will let it guide me. I will forget past mistakes and past failures. Success is my guide today.

MEDITATION SCRIPTURE

"Wealth and riches shall be in his house."

Psalm 112:3b

POINTS TO REMEMBER

1. Today you can get on the journey of success.

2. It is time to do the unthinkable and unimaginable for your life today.

3. Let work become play and your exercise each day.

4. Today bring gain to yourself and satisfaction to others.

5. Forget past mistakes and past failures today.

CHAPTER SIX

MOVE TO REALIZE YOUR DREAM

Affirmation: Today I burn my old bridges and build new ones that others can traverse. Today, I rid myself of "Flat world" people in my life. I stir up the creative powers in me.

At times, you will have to leave the island, country, province and township to release your potential. To release your dream, to release your heart's desire, **just remember the world is your platform.** In this century that we are living, there have been phenomenal improvements in the communication systems and transportation systems of the world. You can get from one place to the next in record time. Success in life is like a marriage. You have never lived with the person before, nor have you experienced the person before. But you had to do some wooing and cajoling to get that spouse. Success is like a marriage in that you would have to leave and cleave. You have to woo success to you. **You would have to leave poverty and marry success.** Leave the state of penury and marry success.

Success is like marriage in that you will have to leave lethargy, laziness and procrastination behind and actually move out of that house and marry success. To succeed takes discipline – at times, getting up early and charting your day. Working until the job is done, spending long hours preparing your vision and plan for your life. The key is work, and work should become pleasure to you. Working your plan leads you inch by inch toward your goal. Actually, what you are doing is climbing up the success ladder.

When I encourage you to move to realize your dream, then you will have to decide on acting on it. Many designers and skilled men and women have left England, China, Germany, Japan and other areas of the world and migrated to the United States and other countries of the world. These people were able to make a success of themselves.

At times the environment that you are in or you have allowed yourself to be a part of keeps you back from realizing your dreams. There comes a time in your life when you have to, as the old adage says, "Burn your bridge behind you." Then you can create new bridges and others can follow you and walk on your bridges to success.

History is replete with many men and women who have relocated from other areas of the world in pursuit of success and the better life.

Christopher Columbus had to move from those negative people around him to discover that the world was not flat, but round. In 1490, Queen Isabella and King Ferdinand of Spain commissioned a royal commission to investigate Christopher Columbus' venture. There were leading geographers and scholars who examined his idea. Their report stated that the plan could not be carried out. They said that the plan was preposterous and impossible. No one living then believed that he could discover a new route to the fabled Indies. Christopher Columbus had problems financing his idea. Columbus ignored the expert's findings. He discovered confidence in Isabella and Ferdinand. Eventually, the Nina, the Pinta and the little Santa Maria set sail and a "flat" world was found to be round. The lands Christopher Columbus discovered became the bridge that others could follow to seize their moment of success. These lands became thriving and bountiful lands. The "impossible" was turned into "the possible."

You have to move to realize your dream. My cousin, Sir Milton Allen, was the first native Governor of one of the islands Christopher Columbus discovered. I lived with him for a few years. He told me that he had to leave his islands of 68 square miles to pursue his dream of a higher education. He attended classes in the evening on effective speaking in New York and he was an avid reader of library books. Then he returned to his island and became the first native Governor of the island.

I am a believer that changing places can give you the chance that you need to change your life for the better, and place you on the road toward realizing success. When you change country or location, you then have the power to choose your friends and break any bad habits that were hindering you from successful thoughts and creativity. You will be able to build that bridge so that others can come and enjoy success with you. But you have to take the first step. The world is your platform.

POWER POINT

Today, I burn my old bridges and build new ones that others can traverse. Today, I rid myself of the "flat world" people in my life. I stir up the creative powers in me.

MEDITATION SCRIPTURE

"I press toward the mark for the prize of the high calling."

Philippians 3:14

POINTS TO REMEMBER

1. The world is your platform.

2. Woo success to you.

3. Leave poverty (state of penury) and marry success.

4. Working your plan leads you inch by inch toward your goal.

5. Today set sail to a new life, a new venture.

6. Changing places can give you a new zeal and a new grasp on life.

7. Today, stir up the creative powers in you that lie dormant.

CHAPTER SEVEN

BE LIKE THE CACTUS

Affirmation: Today, no matter how I feel, no matter what the circumstances are, I will sink my roots down deep and grow where I am and blossom. For out of failure, I will see success. No matter what the circumstances in my life are, I will grow.

Today, no matter how I feel, no matter what the circumstances are, I will sink my roots down and grow where I am and blossom. **Out of failure, I will see success.** No matter what the circumstances are in my life, I will grow and give life. I see a forest. I plant today, seeds of goodness that will mushroom into seeds of greatness.

Once you are alive and doing something, you are apt to experience failure. Many people who succeed in life have failed many times before they realized success. **You must view your failures and problems as opportunities to grow.**

President Lincoln had a streak of failures in his life. He had many reasons in his life to throw in the proverbial towel. Abraham Lincoln's life of failures and success:

Difficult childhood – (Failed)

Less than one year of formal schooling – (Failed)

Failed in business in 1831 – (Failed)

Defeated for Legislature '32 – (Failed)

Again failed in business '33 – (Failed)

Elected to Legislature '34 – (Succeeded)

Fiancée died '35 – (Mourning brokenhearted)

Defeated for speaker '38 – (Failed)

Defeated for elector '40 – (Failed)

Only one of his four sons lived past age 18 (Mourning brokenhearted)

Defeated for Congress '43 – (Failed)

Elected for Congress '46 – (Succeeded)

Defeated for Congress '48 – (Failed)

Defeated for Senate '55 – (Failed)

Defeated for Vice President – (Failed)

Defeated for Senate '58 – (Failed)

Elected President of the United States of America '60 – (Major Success)

Henry Ford, during the development of his first car, forgot to put in a reverse gear in the car. Thomas Edison spent two million dollars on an invention, which proved to be of little value.

Do not allow failure to cause you to stop trying and cause you to lose your momentum in life. Use failure as a **stepping-stone** to success. Today, you can shake yourself out of that failure and out of that depressed state. Once you are breathing the breath of life, you can succeed, and like President Lincoln, stand at your mountain of success and leave an inheritance and a legacy behind and cause change in your surroundings and in the world.

Henry Ford did not scrap his project about his car because the reverse gear was not in the first car. This failure presented an opportunity for him. He then worked on creating a reverse gear that would improve his product. Today, you also can seize the moment and produce success out of failure. Today, the Ford Motor Company is a multi-billion dollar company.

Let your mind work for you. You are a creative person. Let your creative juices flow. Your failure can cause you to succeed and you will learn why you failed. View your failure in a different light. Step off of the platform of failure and into the rushing waters of success.

If Thomas Edison had looked at his failure of spending two million dollars on a product, today civilization would be regressing instead of progressing.

"Out of every adversity comes an equal or greater opportunity." It never fails.

I remember when my brother started in business and the business was doing so well that the owner of the building did not appreciate a young man progressing. He canceled the lease after a few months. My brother was in desperation to locate a building to house the business. However, my brother walked down the block from our business and was inquiring for a place to rent. The first person he inquired of told him of a place that was for sale. We purchased that building. Today, it houses the Glimbaro Guest House, the best guesthouse on the island of St. Kitts.

Out of your adversity let that great opportunity come forth. Purpose in your heart not to sit and invite failure into your day, but be determined to invite positivism into your life. One wise man said, "It is better to aim your arrow at a star and hit an eagle than to aim your arrow at a star and hit a stone."

Get ready today to leave a legacy and an inheritance behind. In 1994, I was preparing my land to build my home. I had my cutlass cutting through the thick forest of trees. I encountered a cluster of cactus plants. I started hacking at them cutting them into small pieces. Several days after, I visited and discovered that a piece of cactus was on its side on a mound of dirt with two healthy shoots about one inch long. I took it up and saw a root system being formed. I then laughed to myself when I saw the survival instincts in this plant. I observed the flat cactus and turned it over on the other side so that the roots were up in the air. Several weeks later, I examined the cactus and discovered that it was on the opposite side and there was no root system, but on the side where the roots were, there were shoots of about one and a half inches.

The cactus was engineered to succeed no matter what the condition was. **The cactus survived on either side.** Be like the cactus, be ready to grow and sink your root down deep and blossom right where you are. If you try, you can make it happen. You see, only you can prevent growth in your life and shut the door of progress in your life. Determine today, no matter what side you are on, to survive and reach out and seize the opportunities that are around you every day and grow.

POWER POINT

Today, no matter how I feel, no matter what the circumstances are, I will sink my roots down deep and grow where I am and blossom. For out of failure, I will see success. No matter what the circumstances in my life are I will grow.

MEDITATION SCRIPTURE

"This is the day which the Lord hath made we will rejoice and be glad in it. Save now, I beseech thee, O Lord: O Lord send now prosperity."

Psalm 118:24-25

POINTS TO REMEMBER

1. Today, plant seeds of greatness that will mushroom into trees of greatness.

2. View your failures and problems as an opportunity to grow.

3. Today you can shake yourself out of that failure and depressed state.

4. Once you are breathing the breath of life, you can succeed.

5. Let your mind work for you. You are a creative person.

6. Step out of failure into success today.

7. Be like the cactus. Succeed no matter what the climate of your life is.

MY CLOSING THOUGHTS

If this book has helped you, I'd love to hear from you! You may order additional copies for your children, friends and associates at your workplace.

The Greatest Gift Of All …Is The Gift Of Wisdom.

You may write the author at:

Oral Hazell

P.O. Box 304283

St. Thomas USVI 00803

To order copies of this book visit or call

Tel: 340-774-5400

www.oralhazellministry.org

Email: oral.hazell@gmail.com

www.ingramcontent.com/pod-product-compliance
Lightning Source LLC
Chambersburg PA
CBHW081123240526
45470CB00019B/2986